The Mind Set of the Investor

By

Omar Seda

Matthew 6:7-8

"Ask, and it will be given it to you;

seek, and you will find; knock, and it

will be opened to you.

For everyone who asks receives, and

and he who seeks finds, and to him who

knocks it will be opened."

Jesus Christ

Acknowledgement

First, I want to give thanks to that all knowing force that binds all things and ideas. It has infinite power especially when applied with will power. Second, I want to thank Attorney Trasha Nicole Hickman, who reminded me that we determine our worth not the world around us. Lastly, I want to thanks my mother who planted the seed of determination in my mind before I understood fully the need for it.

Table of Contents

Introduction

The investor who takes a portion of his or her money and sets it aside is usually thought to be frugal. When I was young, no one told me about investing or saving. Money, like most issues in my family, was a secret. Growing up I discovered quickly the need for money. I came from a family that was neither financially well off nor middle class. I have always loved being in business. My first business endeavor was a lemonade stand that I started because I came from a poor family and none of the kids on the block wanted to play with my brothers, sister or I. The kids in the neighborhood would play touch football or basketball in someone's yard. My need for money helped me develop the idea that if I could not play which is what I wanted to do then I would find another way to hang out with the kids in my neighborhood. I took some lemons from my mother's shelf along with some sugar, a giant igloo cooler and some cups. I sold a cup of lemonade to the kids in the neighborhood for fifty cents. That was my way of developing an idea that would allow me to interact with the kids in my neighborhood. I made twenty dollars in two days, so I decided that every Friday I would sell lemonade to the kids in my neighborhood. I continued this business for two years every summer.

By year three, I grew tired of the lemonade business, so I decided to end that business venture. One of the parents of a kid in the neighborhood saw my determination and befriended me. She asked me to sweep in front of their house which I did. In return, she gave me ten dollars. This was the birth of a new idea and a new business venture for me. I thought there are more lawns than lemonade stands, so I decided that I would mow lawns that summer in the hot sun. In the fall, I decided to rake leaves. Eventually, I had ten customers that I worked for consistently. I continued this business for a couple of year. The money I made from this business was the money that I used to go to the movies and buy snacks. At the time, I never thought to open a savings account at the local bank and no one advised me as a kid to open one. My experience with finance as a kid gave me the desire to teach my kids about financial literary and to provide them with a strong financial education. When I give my kids their allowance, I make them put one-fourth to one-half of it into a savings account. Frequently, I would sit my kids down and show them the salaries of CEOs of major corporations on the internet. They saw three million this and ten million that. The purpose of this exercise was to teach them to aim high and to not settle for eighty thousand or a hundred thousand a year. I wanted them to see that there were people making multimillion dollar salaries and they could too.

Another experience that had a profound impact upon my love for business was my mother opened a small store called The African Shop. I was eager to help, so after school I would go to her store. I did not agree wholeheartedly with some of my mother's thoughts on the look of the store; however, I had no say in how it was operated. This was my formal introduction to business. One day a high school teacher asked me what I wanted to be. Immediately I said a businessman. Not everyone knows during his or her childhood what he or she wants to become. Some people discover their calling later in life. The same is true for investing. Some people are intuitively good at investing while others have to learn how to become good investors. It is my belief that at some point you must drink the Kool-Aid if you are going to be a good investor. There is a mindset that says if you take all the money in the world and divide it evenly among everyone the ones with the most money will end up with it again. I want to teach you how to develop

the mindset of an investor and to develop a mindset of wealth.

Chapter One
The Mindset of the Consumer

There is nothing wrong with being a consumer. After all, it is consumers, who help businesses grow, thrive and evolve. It is consumers who are the demand behind the supply. It is consumers who jump start, invigorate and energizes the economy. Consumers are the heart, soul and life force of the economy. If consumers don't spend money, then the economy as a whole suffers. A consumer is a person who buys cars, boats and other non-income producing things. The problem arises when you use all of your money to buy non-income producing things. In the United States, we consume more than most countries. As a matter of fact, we are responsible for 35% of all items brought around the world. The sad part is that we don't build anything here anymore. With General Motors filing for bankruptcy, one-third of the approximately 15 million cars that

GM produced in the United States will be produced in China and Africa. Africa is the last place that major corporations can go to find cheap labor readily available. Africa is relatively undeveloped and ready for development.

In the house in which I grew up, my parents talked about owning your own business, but they talked little about investing in general and investing in the stock market in particular. It was not until I went to college that I was exposed to families that had stock portfolios. Most people in my neighborhood in my early years had cars and houses. They brought their cars on credit. The purchasing of a house was a different story. In minority neighborhoods, many minorities rented a house. When they went to the bank to get a home loan, the standards were so high that many could not afford a home. The requirement for a down payment was 20% to 50% so buying clothes, shoes and cars was easier. This created a vicious cycle that went on generation after generation. This is where the mindset of a consumer begins. That is why I am committed to teaching my kids about investing and saving money to make sure they have a sound financial foundation. It is a foundation from which I hope they will never stray. Like most kids they want material things now and that is fine. When my oldest daughter was 19 years old, she called my office and asked me to buy her a cell phone. After she asked me to buy her a cell phone, I could see in my mind's eye long phone calls to her friends and big bills to me. I said to her "I have five little words for you may I take your order please." I told her that was a joke, but my words inspired her to go get an after school job. She used the money from her job to purchase a cell phone. As she got older, she confessed to me that having her own money was empowering. To hear her say those words, made me feel good. I continue to send her money for books and the other necessities that she needs for college but for the most part she is independent. Since the banking crash of 2008, we have been forced to rethink how we use our credit and money. There was a time when we could blame our parents for not teaching us how to save or how to invest money, but the truth is the internet and library has taken away all excuses. The consumer is someone who buys things and does not invest or save any of his or her money. As time continues to change, we have to rethink whether investing is enough. There is as much information that is beneficial as there is information that is detrimental to us. The rules have changed but the fundamentals of being a consumer or an investor have not changed. I am not advising anyone not to be a consumer, but I am advising that we add the principle of balance to consuming, spending, saving and investing.

Chapter Two
The Mindset of the Investor

An investor is someone who places her money into an investment and expects to receive more money from the investment than she put into it. When I think of an investor, Warren Buffett comes to mind. Let's think about the kind of mind you need to have to qualify as an investor. A parent who sacrifices a new car so that his child can go to college is an investor. Parents who see their children as undervalued resources and who take the time to invest and reinvest in them are investors. An investment is normally defined as using money to make more money; however, an investment does not have to be limited to finance alone. We could define an investment as anything that adds value or enhances your life. You must define what an investment means to you. To me, sending my kids to college is an investment. Buying twenty acres of land along a highway that is being developed is an investment. An individual who puts change in a jar at the end of the night or who puts change in a jar at the end of the week and wraps it up and deposit the money into a savings account is an investor. An individual who pays herself first is an investor. To pay yourself first, means that when you get your paycheck or commission check the first person who gets paid is you. Yes that rights you not Wells Fargo or Con Edison but **YOU!!!** An individual who pays himself first would buy shares of stock for his portfolio. An individual who purchases bonds is an investor. An individual who purchases shares of stock through a dividend reinvestment programs monthly is an investor.

Principle number one identify your purpose and understand the reason for your purpose. Let's say the child you sent to school decides to drop out after a year and half. God forbid that this should happen. To handle this situation well, you must manage your reaction to the event. In order to manage your reaction, you must direct your thoughts. It is very important not to overreact to negative events. The same holds true for investing. At the time of this writing, there was a major correction in the banking system that has taken place. For example, banks have ceased to lend money freely and foreclosures are happening by the millions. You cannot control what is happening with the banks but you can control how you will act. This economic downturn while bad for most it was a boom for others. If you were a first time homebuyer, there were opportunities to own a home at about half the price in some cases. Without a cool head, you would have missed it. Market corrections in and of themselves are not bad. It is our perception of market corrections that determine our reality. Investors who understand that no matter what conditions are presented that it is their perception of the conditions that matter will always thrive. Inventors who see and believe that market corrections are opportunities to purchase assets at a lower price than normal and who purchase these depreciated assets will always thrive. When you hear negative news in general and negative financial news in particular, choose not to overreact. I love market corrections. All over the news the media told investors stay away from homebuilders. When I looked at some of the homebuilders' stocks they were down big, but their balance sheets were okay. I bought them at three dollars and sold them at seven dollars. The next principle is to think for yourself. Gather the information but choose to think for yourself. If possible, be consistent in thinking. I mean assess your strengths and skills. If you need more knowledge then read more books or take a class. I have been an investor for fifteen years, yet I read at least ten to twenty books a year and that's not counting the hundreds of balance sheets and the thousands of income statements and cash flow statements that I read. Ask yourself the question "Am I an investor?" You are the only one who can answer that question. If you are not sure, work with a broker. A good broker will guide and protect you from some of the really challenging investments strategies like margin or options because they are cheap. Margin is not a bad thing in and of itself, but used incorrectly it can wipe you out. The same thing is true with options used correctly it is a great tool for hedging your position, but if it is misused it could crush you. Margin is when you take an amount of money let's say $5000.00. You want to buy $10,000.00 worth of stock. You would go to your broker and sign a margin agreement and you would get a line of credit of an additional $5000.00 with interest. Some firms will let you borrow as much as $2000.00 which is usually the minimum amount. Options are a contract between two parties that give the buyers and sellers the right, but not the obligation to buy or sell

an asset at a price on or before a specific future date.

Chapter Three
Tax Sale

A tax sale is when you owe taxes to the county on a piece of property, and the county auctions the property to pay the delinquent taxes. Before the property is sold at a tax sale, a person has an opportunity to pay off the taxes that are owed along with the penalty and interest. If he or she does not pay the taxes before the tax sale then, the county will sale the property for delinquent taxes. If the property is sold at a tax sale, the original owner of the property will have an opportunity to redeem the property during the redemption period. The redemption period is the time set by the law in the state in which the property was sold to redeem the property after it has been sold at a tax sale. During the redemption period, the county pays interest on the amount of the bid of the successful bidder. The amount of interest the county pays is determined by the law in the state in which the tax sale occurred. If the owner of the property redeems the property by paying the taxes owed along with the interest and penalty, the county will void the sale for that particular piece of property and pay the successful bidder his or her principal plus interest. However, if the property is not redeemed for taxes, then in some states a tax deed will be issued and in other states a tax lien certificate will be given to the successful bidder. If someone purchases property in a state that issues tax deeds and the property is not redeemed then the county will issue a tax deed to the successful bidder. After a tax deed is issued, a lawsuit will need to be brought to clear the title to the property which is known as foreclosing. When you clear the title to a piece of property, you are bringing a lawsuit to remove the names of all persons or entities who have or may claim to have an interest in the property. However, if you purchase property in a state that issues tax lien certificates, the county will not issue you a tax deed. The county will give you a tax lien certificate that pays you interest according to state law. I attended a tax sale in Atlanta with my business partner. The day of the tax sale it was cold because it was the first part of April and spring had not arrived. When all of a sudden to my surprise, protesters came out of nowhere. In Atlanta, they hold tax sales on the court house steps. The protesters were screaming where is the American Dream you could hardly hear a word the auctioneer was saying. I did not leave Atlanta with any property, but I turned to my partner and said great we are in an episode of Frasier. This was during the banking correction of 2008 and 2009. Principle number three is watch your spending. Please don't buy more assets than your wallet can handle. Buying assets is a great thing. For example, let's say you purchase a house. Please remember there are taxes and insurance and other cost that are associated with the maintenance of a house unless your goal is short term. By short term, I mean selling it very shortly after your purchase it. This process is call flipping. The times we live in have a tendency to make people and investors fearful. The fear that I am talking about is the fear of loss. You have to take chances to get a return, but you must also use your best judgment.

There is an adviser who has a client who is having money problems. The client has credit card bills pilling up and she is a month behind on her mortgage. In addition, the client has a desire to paint her house because it sustained water damage. Two years earlier the financial advisor sold her an annuity. Now she needs money. The adviser had the nerve to advise her against withdrawing money from the annuity. The woman called me she did not know what do. As we talked for a while, I discovered she had four whole life policies which totaled twenty thousand dollars. I suggested that she borrow some of the money from the cash value of one of the policies to pay the mortgage and borrow some money from the cash value of the other policy to take care of her other needs. She could have gone into foreclosure. Many people aren't so lucky. I fault her adviser because she was fearful and did not put her client's needs first. My point is to know your whole financial picture and know your adviser. She could have made the decision not to use the policy out of fear. I thought it was sound advice. She opened an account with me and she has been a client of mine for seven years now. If you want to withdraw money from your annuity, all you need to do is call customer service, give them your account number and tell them to cash out a part or your entire annuity and mail you a check. Many annuity products promise you monthly payments after you turn fifty nine and a half that's their appeal. The problem is that things happen that may cause you to need to use some of the money in the annuity. Make sure to ask your adviser if something happens and you need the money what would you do? What is the procedure to exit the annuity? Technically your adviser is supposed to tell you how to liquidate the annuity if you need to do so as well as the limitations of annuities. Although some advisers are afraid to discuss the limitations of annuity, out of fear of losing the sale. The adviser should talk to you about the benefits and the costs that's what a good adviser does. Please consult your financial adviser to discuss the tax consequences of withdrawing money from your annuity.

Chapter Four
Not All Southern Women Know Voodoo

I went through a couple of training programs at firms on WallStreet. Some of the training programs were good. The good ones wanted you to have licenses in insurance and asset management. The idea was to retrieve assets and the firm would pool the money into a mutual fund so the fund managers could manage it. The firm would give you a list of questions to ask the prospect and then ask for an order. Then there were the other firms. They trained you to use high pressure tactics. The work day started at 7:30 am and we were on the phone by 8:00 am. We were handed a written script and our goal for the day was get 10 leads. By leads, I mean good prospects. If we didn't get 10 leads, our broker humiliated us in front of the broad room. The worst part of the experience was that we were there for 12 hours on our feet screaming in the phone and made

$150.00 per week. We had eight weeks to complete the program. After that, the broker stopped paying the draw and we had to build a book of business of our own and give the broker fifteen accounts. Needless to say some brokers we ended up working for were quite sneaky and others were down right cruel. When I started, I was shy. I was uncomfortable yelling at the top of my lungs pushing people for information about assets, net worth and so on. It was there I had the good fortune of meeting John Tyus around 1997. John was excellent at sales. Once I became a registered broker I had to get 15 accounts for my broker to go on my own. Most guys had scripts that they read like robots as soon as a prospect got on the phone. The problem was when the guy or gal was asked questions about the stock he or she could not answer unless his or her broker was listening in and feeding him or her answers. John was different. He made me read the facts about the company, namely, the company's balance sheet, earning per share and where the company was located. To this day, I continue to use this technique; however, I have fine-tuned it and added some additional information when evaluating a company. When I got my first account on the phone, the prospect asked about ten questions about the stock I answered all of them. The client stopped talking at this point and John listened to our conversation. I was about to talk and John signaled me not to talk. I did not understand what he was doing. The prospect was deciding whether or not to buy if I had talked I would have over sold him on the stock. Five minutes elapsed and we sat there on the phone silent as a tomb. The prospect said how much is 100 shares. I gave the price for 100 shares of stock along with the cost of my commission. Then the client said let's buy a 100 shares, but I surprised John. I said I think you should buy 300 shares. I proceeded to explain why I thought the prospect should buy 300 shares. I told the prospect the stock could make a 20% to 25% increase then we can sell half of the shares and I could send the principal back to you and work with the profits. This would diminish the client's risk. The client agreed. Later that day John told me I took an awful risk. He said the client could have said no altogether. I told him I felt like the client liked the stock. To this day, I take risks. In 2011, I have expanded the practice to Columbia, South Carolina a risky move. Upon doing my research, I discovered Columbia, South Carolina is one of fastest growing cities in the country. I wanted to be there before the crowd arrived. South Carolina is where I choose to start buying land. Land ownership is and will continue to be an important component of any investment portfolio. This is what makes South Carolina important to me and should make it important to you. Find your own South Carolina. Perhaps you might like Ohio or Arizona. The guiding principle is to take some risk not just in business but in love and in your career. Choose to pursue whatever you want. Growing up I was told so many things about the South none of them were true. I had to go there and experience it for myself. It is like that in investing. The internet, newspapers and cable media have a lot of ways of making people fearful. To combat the fear, do your own research or find a good broker that you trust and ask him what is true and what is fiction? There are some truths about the South the no one had to tell me. For instance, the food in the South is great. The myths about the South regarding education and business are not true. Religion is a very important part of the fabric of the South but not to the point that you will be chased out of town if you don't attend church every Sunday. When you hear fearful information about investing, do your own research and investigation, think critically and independently and make an informed decision that is right for you. After all, all southern women don't know voodoo. It is true where there is smoke there is fire but not all fires are a bad

thing.

Chapter Five
Catching a Cloud

Catching a cloud is a term that skydivers use. I am not a sky diver although I would like to try it. As you jump out of the airplane, there is a mist of air and as you go through it that is catching a cloud. You probably have to do it to know what it feels like. With respect to investing, catching a cloud means something different. When I talk about catching a cloud, I am referring to buying a stock at a low price and selling it for a substantially higher price. For example, buying a stock at $4.00 and selling it at $20.00. There is no feeling like it. Once you catch a cloud you realize the power of the stock market and what can happen overnight. A bank Certificate of Deposit (CD) cannot increase in value like stocks. Four years ago I bought a company called Dendreon Corporation. Its symbol is DNDN. I am not telling you to buy this company. I am using this company as an example to illustrate a point. At the time that I brought Dendreon Corporation, they were developing a hormone therapy drug for advanced prostate cancer. There was not a drug like it out on the market. Dendreon Corporation received the U.S. Food and Drug Administration (FDA) approval and the stock went from $4.00 to $20.00. That was a big day for my company and one of the many clouds that I have had the good fortune of catching. The question is how do we find these stocks? Here are some of the things I look for in a stock. First, take a look at what the company does. Is it a fast food company? If so, what do they do? Do they sell hamburgers? Look for their competition. If it is a technology company, ask yourself is their technology keeping up with the trends that consumers want? Let's say that we are looking at a cell phone maker. We want to know if the company is producing cell phones that people want. Technology changes so rapidly it is tough to keep up. Second, look at the balance sheet of a company. The balance sheet will show you the gross income and liabilities of the company. If you look at a company's balance sheet and you notice that the last four years and every year after that the company's revenue appear to be sliding that may be a sign that the company is heading for trouble. You will want to investigate further to determine whether you want to invest in this company. The same holds true if you are looking at a company's balance sheet and you notice that its revenue is increasing each year and they have been keeping their expenses down that could turn out to be the goose that lays the golden egg. Ask yourself is the improved revenue because of new products or maybe new management. Call the company and ask for an annual report. If it is a publicly traded company, they will send you an annual report because this is public information. Third, look at the income statement. The income statement will tell you how much money a company earned over a period of time. Also it will show how much money a company spends on research and development. Research and development is important if you are looking at biotech companies. Biotech companies make their money on products that receive FDA approval. In addition, the income statement looks at the operating expense of a company. Operating expense is what it cost a business to stay in business every year. I have given you a few tools to help you get started. If you have additional questions, you can email me at <u>omarseda@aol.com</u>. Take these tools and make them your own. It is my hope and desire that you find your own cloud to catch.

Chapter Six
Employment Does Not Equal Ownership

The problem with employment in 2011 is there is a lack of it.

About twenty-five years ago, I worked as well as ran a business

in the garment industry. At that time, the International Ladies'

Garment Workers' Union was the union that represented that

industry. Around 1987, a new trend started occurring in the

garment industry. Manufacturers started going to Hong Kong to

have garments made. They started manufacturing smaller items

at first and then graduated to having all their sewing done

overseas. As a result, the garment industry in America shrank

and it happened quickly. Next, the manufacturers started going

to China for cheap labor to produce their products. As I reflect

on this trend, I realize that Hong Kong was the broker. The real

work was being done in China. Hong Kong is the broker

connecting Asia with the West. In the 1930s, Arm and Hammer

was one of the first businesses to go to China. In 2011, the majority of the manufacturing is done overseas. I don't think that manufacturing as we know it is coming back soon. For example, Americans that used to work in the textile factories that produced garments have to reeducate themselves or start a business of their own. America has been the leader in innovation. I believe this innovation will be the key. When you own your own business, you have real ownership. You have to work or else the work won't get done but it is worth the effort. If you want to own your own business choose something you like or always wanted to do, then do some research and just do it. In every work environment, there are positives and negatives. Choose to focus on the positives of your work environment. In some work environments, employers treat their employees like they own them. Employment does not equal ownership. From the perspective of the employee, you do not own the company for which you work. Although you don't own the company, you can become an owner of the company if it is a publicly traded company. If you work for a publicly traded company, choose to purchase shares of stock in the company for which you work in your IRA, 401(k) or individual stock account. This will give you an ownership interest in the company. Once you own shares of stock in the company it gives you the opportunity to have a say in how the company is run. If you do not work for a publicly traded company, that does not mean that you should not investment in your company's retirement program. When your employer makes a contribution to your retirement plan, choose to participate. By that I mean, put some of your own money into your retirement account to match the contribution. Whether you work for a publicly traded company or not you should do a great job because you have an incentive in keeping the business operating well. In fact, it means that you should use the job as a stepping stone to a greater position or use it to hone your skills

for the day that you start your own business. If your employer is

mistreating you, don't take it personally. He or she is the one

with the problem. Choose to add value to the work place and if

you feel that you can no longer add value move on to another

job that will respect and appreciate your gifts and talents or start

your own business. While working for someone else continue to

invest in yourself by educating yourself. Employment does not

equal ownership. From the perspective of an employer, you do

not own the people who choose to work with you. If you choose

to treat your employees like property rather than as assets, you

are doing a disservice to your business and your customers.

First, your employees will resent you and they will have less of

an incentive to be productive. Second, they will choose to

withhold valuable ideas that could improve your business and

make it more profitable. Third, they will be less inclined to

35

share solutions to problems that need to be fixed. Don't cut your nose off to spite your face. You could lose some talented workers to your competitor. Choose to invest in the education of your employees because an investment in your employees is an investment in your company.

I think the American labor markets are ready to go to work and have healthy attitudes about it. I think this is going to present major challenges for the unions. They will have to adjust to the new labor markets. For example, the unions pressured GM for 3% raises for their union members every three years to keep up with inflation. I am not saying this is right or wrong it was the way things were done. In 2008, there was a major correction suddenly GM was on the verge of going out business. Consequently, GM had to close plants across the country in some cases twenty thousand people were laid off all at once. The government had to bail them out. As a result, the unions came up with the idea of ownership in GM. They took a 17% stake in GM that was smart. This worked out well, but one-third of GM's manufacturing is done in China. Those jobs won't be back so the employees who were laid off have to reeducate themselves in a new field. The unions will have to learn how to negotiate now that they know the real numbers of GM.

Chapter Seven
Knowing When to Release an Asset

There comes a time when you have to be honest about an investment the same holds true for love and relationships. The question becomes when do you accept the fact that it is time to let go? It is no easier in a personal relationship than it is with the stock market. The difference is with the stock market you can put a stop lose on your down side. Let's say you buy a stock at nine dollars and it goes to seven. It might be time to be honest and say that if the stock declines to six dollars you will sell it. In a relationship, you go on many dates and then you may discover this person is not right for you or you may find out this person is prefect for you so start to build a relationship. This is the difference between a personal relationship and the stock market. When you are at nine dollars and good fortune smiles down on you and the stock goes to fifteen, you take your profits. It is time to let go of that stock and find another stock you like. That is a good ending when you take profit. Let's look at things another way. You bought the stock at nine dollars and fundamentally there is nothing wrong with the stock. The market corrects that is when the market goes down and your nine dollar stock pulls back to six dollars you can cut your losses and sell the stock that is one option; however, you loved the stock at nine you should be pounding the table at six and buying more. If I have a stock position that I think will be a top performer in a year and the market pulls back that's the time to get more stock and bring my cost average down and to purchase the stock at a cheaper price. I will give you an example. I like Visa. The symbol for the stock is V. I am not telling you to buy this stock. At the time of this writing, Visa is an eighty seven dollar stock. I believe by the first quarter of next year it will be a one hundred twenty five dollars stock. In 2011, the United

States got its first downgrade by Standard & Poor's (the S&P rating agency) and the Dow Jones pulled back five hundred points in one day. The next day it pulled back four hundred points. Visa pulled back to seventy four dollars. Some people would panic and sell it. I bought more stock in Visa. Fundamentally there was nothing wrong with Visa. Two weeks later Visa was right back at eight five dollar a share. Not all stocks that you buy behave that way. Some go to six and next stop at four. Before you buy your stock, look at the numbers. If you know you have a good company, buy on the dips by that I mean buy on the lows of the stock. Let's talk about my mistakes I have made in the stock market. One mistake was a stock called Visign. The symbol for the company was VGSN. They made semiconductor chips. I'm not telling to buy this stock or sell it if you own it. I bought VGSN at seven dollars the market corrected and it went to four dollars this was in 2001. At the time when I bought the company, there was nothing fundamentally wrong with the company. The problem was the sector in which the company was located was being flooded with cheap semiconductor chip coming out of Asia. As the year progressed, it became more difficult for them to meet their quarterly numbers. That should have been the time to release that asset, but I went into hope and pray mode that it would come back. The writing was really on the wall when the market ran and VGSN just sat there. That was the time to sell that stock and join in the big bull run that was taking place over a period of a year. I should have sold that stock and found something else to buy. There you have it. Take a look at your portfolio and make some decisions about your stocks or e-mail me at omarseda@aol.com. I will respond. If I can advise you I will, or I will refer you to someone who can.

Chapter Eight
Taxes

You should never let taxes be a reason not to buy or sell a stock. Here are two reasons when it is advantageous to sell a stock for tax purposes. First, the IRS will allow you to take a thirty day tax loss. The thirty day tax loss is when you sell a stock at a loss then wait thirty days and buy it back. This is perfectly legal. Second, is if you have too many capital gains in another part of your portfolio and you have to balance your books by taking a loss. There are additional reasons the IRS will allow you to take a loss but these are the two most popular ones.

Employment has taken the center stage since the government has passed the Restore Employment Act (Hire), IR-2010-33. According to the new law, employers who hire workers during February 3, 2010 to January 1, 2011 may qualify for a 6.2% payroll deduction. This particular program may be over but it has been revived in a similar form. Contact the IRS for more information. They will send you information on what tax laws are available. The unemployment issue is far from over with the middle class being hit the hardest. Currently, the national unemployment rate is 9%. Middle class African American communities have been severely impacted by the economic downturn. Unemployment in some African American communities is higher than 11.2%. There are plenty of talented people from all walks of life who have been affected by the economic downturn. We are all in the same boat. Here is another twist. The unemployed are competing with the underemployed. The underemployed are the part time workers who want full employment. Remember a lot of businesses won't give health insurance to part time workers because the employer has to pay part of the health insurance. If the employer does not have to do that the company saves money.

Let's discuss briefly healthcare reform. Starting in 2014, all Americans will have to have healthcare. Some people say this is unfair, but remember you can't drive a car without insurance. You can't buy a new house without home owners insurance. While I understand the concerns about mandatory health insurance, I think we would all benefit if we were allowed to pick health insurance in any state like car insurance. I think this is an issue for the Supreme Court someday. Health care reform will end up before the Supreme Court because the courts of each state have interpreted the new law differently. Some courts have ruled the new law unconstitutional while others have ruled that it is constitutional. There has to be some uniformity regarding universal healthcare and for that to happen the Supreme Court will have to decide whether the law is constitutional or unconstitutional. The reason I address this issue is because some day it will be a standard withholding like

Social Security (FICA), Medicare (MED) then you will see HETH, for healthcare or something along that line. From a taxpayer perspective it will affect you, but it is a necessary deduction. You may want to check with your current healthcare provider to see what information they can send you or go on the internet and Goggle it. At some point, there will be some changes in the tax code, I believe our government will be between a rock and a hard place and be forced to raise taxes. Many people believe a flat tax will only help the rich, no matter what tax structure you put in place the rich will benefit because they are rich. I think that adding a flat tax along with the current system is the best. I believe the people should decide what tax system works best for them. Now, when I refer to the rich I am talking about people who make one hundred million or more.

If you find yourself unemployed, you may want to withdraw money from your IRA. If you are older than 59½ you qualify for a distribution. You won't pay a penalty for early distribution but you will have to pay federal taxes and state taxes. The good news is at that age your tax rate will be lower than someone less than 59½. Your rate should be about 17%. Double check that number with your accountant to make sure. The reason why is because you current income has a lot to do with it.

If you inherit an IRA, there are different rules that apply depending on whether you are a spouse or a non-spouse. If you are a spouse, you have the option of rolling the money from the inherited IRA over into your name. If the spouse chooses to roll the inherited IRA over into his or her name, taxes rules of IRAs still apply. If you are a non-spouse, you cannot roll the IRA over into your name. You must retitle the account in the name of the deceased for the benefit of the beneficiary. For example, John Doe, deceased for the benefit of Mary Roe, beneficiary. For more information regarding taxes and inherited IRA talk to your accountant.

If the deceased person has a 401k, and you are the beneficiary you may be able to take loans out, but there are tax consequences. Check with your plan because some plans will not let you take money out until you are 59½. Please check with your broker or the plan administrator. I have given you an overview if you e-mail me at omarseda@aol.com with your questions I will go more in depth. As an aside, if you are no longer working at your job, you can roll over your 401k into your IRA. Again check with your broker he or she will tell you the rules and provide you with the paper work.

Chapter Nine
A Wealthy State of Mind

Buy low and sell high we hear that principle of investing all the time. It isn't until you are in a nasty market correction that you realize holy cow this is real money that you could lose then the fear kicks in. If you are fearful, you will be tempted to give into fear. A wealthy state of mind is a positive mind. The first thing you want to do is to begin to eliminate fear and worry. Fear is the cause of so much unhappiness, so many let downs and so many failures. I know that you have been told that about fear or that at least you have heard that fear is the habit of negative thinking. The good news is you can free yourself the same way you use negative affirmations you can turn those thoughts to positive affirmations. One of the best ways is to use positive statements. Don't use statements that put yourself down or anyone else for that matter. The problem with fear is it does not help you get away from the thing you are afraid of or to overcome fear. In order to overcome fear, hold in your mind the positive thoughts until they become a part of your everyday thinking. Remember negativity can only get in through an unguarded subconscious. You may want to know how this relates to investments well for one thing if you have a fear of selling stocks for a chance to buy better stocks you may not do it. The reason is fear never stays in one part of your life it creeps into every part of your life. For instance, once you entertain fear then you are afraid to ask for the raise you deserve or start the business you always wanted to or move to a state where jobs are plentiful. Please understand that fear and worry has never helped anyone. It never has and it never will. Now, once you start to chase fear and worry away they will try to fight to stay this is where your faith kicks in. You will develop your faith because you are no longer worried. In Matthews 17:20,

Jesus said to them, "because of your unbelief, for assuredly I say to you, if you have faith as a mustard seed you will say to this mountain, move from here to there and it will move and nothing will be impossible for you." This is not a Bible lesson but the point is if you only have a little faith you can do great things in your life so image what would happen with complete faith. You know how small a mustard seed is and the seed grows into a big plant. The subconscious mind has unlimited resources at its disposal and it does not matter if someone else is doing great emotional or financially you can do great also. There is plenty for everyone. All you have to do is feed your mind positivity and out comes great new inventions or even stock quotes all available to you for the asking. Let's call this right thinking because it comes from your subconscious mind. Now think of your conscious mind like the gate keeper. Its job is to keep out unwanted thoughts so when you find your being fearful about investing or even passing judgment on someone you don't know because they are different make yourself stop by saying "I'm not going to be negative or judgmental." Instead of saying "I am not afraid" say with bravado "I am full of courage there is nothing to fear" and keep re-enforcing those statements in your subconscious mind and in time fear will leave. Remember to walk courageously, speak courageously, act courageously and will you attain what you are going after. I met a gentleman at a seminar he was afraid of investing in the stock market. His thought on investing in the stock market was it was not safe. His objective was protecting his principal, but he loves the returns that the stock market gives when it runs, so I asked him what he was buying? He said CD's that stands for certificate of deposits from a bank where he held a checking account. Then I ask him what rate the CD was paying him? It was a six month CD with a 5% return on it. I told him that is a great rate, but remember that is the stated rate that is not your actual rate. He asked me to explain the difference between the stated rate and the actual rate. I said first you must include the hidden inflation number which is about 3% a year then remember those assets have to be managed by someone so add another 1% to that then at some point you have to pay capital gain to the IRS on the 5% each year. The bank will mail you a 1099 at the end of the year so you are really getting something like 1% when you look at it closely. I put together a portfolio that gave him preservation of most of his principal with some speculation for better returns on his money that was seven years ago and he is still a client of mine to this day. The point is do not let fear stop you from looking for bigger returns because they are out there and don't let fear stop you from investing.

Chapter Ten
Legal

I want to tell you a story about a broker dealer that I was with as an independent broker. We can call the broker dealer a platform. At first things were working out nicely, but after six years they found themselves in legal problems because of their need to have heavy hitters on the platform. This group tried to sell a private placement that was not fully registered. I am not mad at them. Every broker dealer wants to grow their firm but at what cost. Every broker dealer wants brokers who will open five million dollar accounts and higher. There is nothing wrong with that it is just the way of the industry. Every broker dealer wants brokers that will do a million dollars a month; however, some of their brokers are developing and growing nicely but they are not doing a million dollars a month. My thought is that being patient allows the broker to develop a good relationship with the client and the broker dealer (B/D) to develop a good relationship with the broker. This allows the broker and the broker dealer to grow. Why is this important to you? This is important to you because suitable products and caring service is all but gone in this industry. At some point FINRA, who is the governing body over brokers, ruled against the broker dealer and they were asked to pay the clients their money back and they were fined close to a million dollars. They ended up shutting down. There were clients, who for whatever reason would not their take their money out so when the doors shut the Securities Investors Protection Corporation (SIPC) had to step in and provide insurance up to $500,000.00 net equity balance including $250,000.00 in cash. In order to collect a claim, the investor must show that the loss arose from the insolvency of the broker dealer and not because of fraud, misrepresentation or bad investments. What would happen if this happened to you? You would receive a letter giving you a certain amount of time to turn in your claim form. Then you would need to fill out the claim form or ask your accountant to help you with it because they would know your stock positions. If the claim form is not filled out properly, SIPC will refuse to pay the claim. If you fill out your claim form incorrectly, you would have to send a letter stating why your claim should not be denied. Remember to have supporting documents, your past statements and any letters from the broker dealer. Now the Federal Deposit Insurance Corporation (FDIC) is another independent agency created by the United States Congress pursuant to the Glass-Steagall Act of 1933. The FDIC provides deposit insurance. The agency guarantees safety deposits of its member banks currently up to $250,000.00 per client. It supervises and checks for the safety and soundness of certain financial institutions some of which are brokerage firms. Additionally, the FDIC performs certain consumer protection functions and manages banks that fall into receivership. Receivership is when a bank fails. Insured institutions are required to place signs in there window that they are insured. In the 2008 banking correction, banks that failed had what was called mortgage back securities. Mortgage back securities are the mortgages of home owners that are bundled into a bond called a Commercial Mortgage Obligations (CMO). Commercial Mortgage Obligations in of themselves are not bad, but when rating agencies gave them a AAA rating it allowed the banks to borrow against the bond(s) in some cases as much as 90%. Borrowing is what caused all the problems of the banking crash. Another factor was that a lot of mortgage companies sold what's call interest only mortgages which allowed homeowners to pay only the interest on their loans. The mortgage companies encouraged the brokers to sell interest only adjustable rate mortgages because the commission for interest only loans was bigger than the commission for fixed rate mortgages. This occurred during the time interest rates were increased to 5.25% so instead of paying an $800.00 a month mortgage it increased to $1,200.00 which was out of the reach of most consumers' budget and many defaulted on their loans. It was a house of cards built on sand. The consumer defaulted, then the bank foreclosed on the consumer, it caused the bonds to lose value, when the bonds lost value the banks were in trouble because they had margin against the bonds so the value of bonds came down, then the banks had a margin calls and that forced the banks to sell these bonds at a fraction of their costs. Some of the bank had to go into receivership. This forced Congress to enact financial regulatory reform. Normally, the decision to deem a financial firm as failing would be decided by the FDIC and the Federal Reserve. There are some exceptions when neither the FDIC nor the Federal Reserve decides if a financial institution is failing. For instance, if it a broker dealer or large subsidiary of a broker dealer is failing, then the Securities and Exchange Commission (SEC) not the FDIC will make the final determination. The FDIC will be consulted once the determination is made and would become the receiver. Another exception is if the financial institutions are insurance companies then the state regulators are charged with resolving the issue under state law. If the state regulators do not resolve the issue within 60 days, the FDIC will step in at that time. I have broad stroked this so if you want a complete explanation or more information you can look it up or e-mail me at omarseda@aol.com. I would be more than happy to provide you with as much information as you require or show you where you can get more information.

Chapter Eleven
To Refinance or Not to Refinance that Is the Question

Refinancing is when you replace an existing debt obligation with another debt obligation under different terms. As a result of the banking collapse in 2008, foreclosures skyrocketed and the government was forced to step in and lay down some grounds rules. In the past, it was considered a good time to refinance when the mortgage dropped under 2% of your existing rate. A drop in interest rate is a good factor for refinancing. There are other good reasons for refinancing. For example, when your income has increased or when your credit history has improved the best rates are typically given to borrowers with the best credit scores. If you have paid off a debt like a car loan, your debt to income ratio will improve as a result you will most likely qualify for a much better interest rate. Another reason to refinance is when you have an adjustable rate mortgage and you want switch to a fix rate mortgage. This is a great reason to refinance. Now let's talk about the negatives of refinancing. I believe that your home is your number one asset. A number of books will disagree with me. Consolidating debt is one of the most dangerous financial moves a home owner can make. At first glance, paying off a high interest rate loan with a low interest rate mortgage may seem smart, but the homeowner is transferring unsecured debt into debt that is secured by their home. For example, if home owners refinance to pay off their credit cards, they may be tempted to reuse the credit cards after they pay them off. If they are unable to meet their payments, they will face foreclosure. Another reason that refinance is bad is that many homeowners may be tempted to move to a longer term loan. For example, if you have fourteen years left to pay off your home and you refinance to obtain a lesser rate, the banks will give you a thirty year mortgage unless you ask for a shorter term. In essence, you will pay more money because you are starting over. Instead of having fourteen years left to pay off your loan you now have thirty years to pay it off. Lastly, if you refinance your home to get cash to invest this idea in and of itself is not a bad idea, but only if you are disciplined and will truly use the money for investing. The problem is when most people get the cash it is easy to run through it. Besides paying down a 6% loan is better than buying a CD at 2% at some bank. If you have a good broker that you trust, then I can see this or if you are savvy enough, then you can take the gamble.

Elizabeth Warren is on the Financial Products Safety Commission. The mission of this commission is to eliminate the tricks and the traps that fooled so many homeowners. Ms. Warren is a Harvard Law Professor and Chairwoman of the Congressional Oversight Panel which supervises the Treasury's management of Troubled Asset Relief Program (TARP). Ms. Warren has written or co-authored fifteen books and she reviews financial regulations. The biggest problem homeowners' face is how to refinance their homes that have dropped substantially in value. This is also an issue facing the government. Remember these homeowners have kept up with their payments the value of their homes has dropped substantially due to no fault of their own. Hopefully, the homeowners are able to take advantage of these low fix rates which will reduce their cost. President Obama is currently working on a plan to answer the question how do you refinance an underwater mortgage? There are a lot of websites you can go to and obtain estimates like www.housevalues.com if want to know the current value of your home and land. Also you can contact the Assessor's Office in your state and ask them the value of your home or land. The Assessor's Office assesses real property and varies from state to state.   If you need to refinance, knowing the value of your property is important.   If your current home is less than what you paid for it, there is a program called Home Affordable Refinance Program (HARP) that may be able to help you.   The program helped far less homeowners than the White House thought it would.   The program was set up for homeowner who cannot qualify for a loan from private companies.   The White House hoped that millions would benefit from this program but so far approximately 800,000 have benefitted from it.   My thought is that if more people knew it was available more would apply.   Another reason more people have not benefitted from the program is because there are stricter income requirements. Stimulating the housing market is a very important part of moving the economy forward that is why it so important that we try to keep people in their homes.   President Obama proposed recently a $15 billion dollar plan to fix up foreclosed homes in areas that has been hit the hardest. For every home sold, there

are several jobs created.

Chapter Twelve
Insurance

Insurance is money that is used to replace the income of the person who has passed away. Insurance allows the survivors to maintain their standard of living or raise it substantially. There are two types of insurance. The first type of insurance is term insurance. Term is life insurance that provides coverage at a fixed rate or an increasing rate for a definite time. Term life insurance is the least expensive way to purchase life insurance with substantial death benefits. Term is good if you are on a budget. Remember it does not build equity and when you get to end of your term which varies from 20, 30 or 35 years you will have to renew at a much higher rate. Some term policies have a return of premium rider attached to them. A term life insurance policy with a return of premium rider allows the policy owner to receive a portion of the premium if the insured outlive his or her term. Ask your life insurance agent about whether they offer a term insurance policy with a return of premium rider. For instance, if you purchase a 20 year term policy and you outlive the term, then the insurance company will give you back a portion of the money you paid each month for the last twenty years if the policy has a return of premium rider. Term life insurance is pure insurance. It has no saving component attached to it. Primerica Life Insurance Company coined the phrase "Buy Term Invest the Difference." Buy Term Invest the Difference means that you can purchase a term policy for an inexpensive amount and invest the remainder of the money that you are saving each month into a mutual fund. However, this principle can be applied to other investment vehicles. You can buy a term policy and invest the remainder of the money that you are saving in stocks, bonds, cmo, and high yield bonds. Here you can finally have your cake and eat it too, namely insurance and investments. The downside of term insurance is that if your insurance company does not offer a return of premium and you outlive your term, you have no insurance.

The second type of insurance is whole life. Whole life is a life insurance policy that remains intact for the whole life of the insured. This type of policy is a life insurance policy with a saving account component. A good point is it has an investment component which is useful. The insurance companies invest the money in bonds, money market or even stocks. The policy builds cash value you can borrow against, and you can lock in the same monthly payment over the life of the policy. Another benefit of whole insurance is that the money in your cash value grows tax deferred. An additional, benefit of whole life is that it forces you to save money because a portion of the premium pays for the insurance and the remainder goes into the cash value which is a saving account. At first glance you may think, great I can save an extra $60 a month. Well not really there are expenses. The $60 disappears in commissions and expenses for the first three years. After that, the return will be 2.6%. The average mutual fund has a return of is .07%. There are some negatives to whole life policies. First, if you die, unlike buy term and invest the difference where your family would get both the insurance and your investment, with whole life your family would only get the face amount of the policy. If you die, your family won't get both the savings and the face amount of the policy. The savings goes to the insurance company. If you live and you borrow money from your policy, then you have to pay it back with interest at a rate that is higher than what the insurance company was paying you when you put the money in your cash value. If you don't pay the money that you borrowed back, then the insurance company will deduct the money from you cash value and once your cash value hits zero your policy will lapse. Lastly, if you take all of your money out of your cash value, then your policy will lapse. With whole life, you can't have your cake and eat it too. I am not saying whole life is a bad idea, I just want you know the good, the bad, and the ugly. Now that you are knowledgeable about insurance remember it is an important component of any financial portfolio. You want to know that your family is protected financially. You need to purchase enough insurance to do the following things: bury your loved one, payoff the mortgage, payoff the debts of the deceased love one, provide for your children's education and provide your family with enough money to live. I have tried to give the positive and the negative sides of insurance. Make sure that you have some kind of insurance in place. Make sure to add a disability rider/waiver of premium in the event you get injured on job so that your policy will not lapse.

Chapter Thirteen
Debt Consolidation and Your Credit Score

Debt consolidation is taking out one loan to pay off other loans. This is usually done to secure a low fix rate. Debt consolidation is an unsecured loan paying off other unsecured loans. Refinancing is a form of debt consolidation. Today most debt consolidation is secured by an asset like a mortgage of a house so if you default on the consolidated deal they can force you into foreclosure so be mindful when you go into this kind of agreement. A good thing about your debt consolidator is they will call your creditors on your behalf and get your debt reduced to 20% to 50% on the dollar in some cases. Debt consolidation combines your various debts into one payment at a lower rate which will give you the breathing room you need each month. I believe that debt consolidation is a good idea especially if you have high interest rate credit cards. Also debt consolidation can be good for student loans that last for years. If the debtor is near

bankruptcy, the consolidator can discount his or her costs.

Remember to shop around to find the best consolidator. Before

you take advantage of debt consolidation, ask questions. If you

find you need to file bankruptcy, go head and file there is no

shame in it. There are warning signs that you need to take

advantage of debt consolidation like your credit score. A credit

score is a numerical expression based on a statistical analysis of

a person's credit files. What is good credit score? A credit

score of 700 is decent. A credit of 800 or higher is golden.

Let's say your credit score is 550 which is bad and you want to

improve it. The first thing I would say is keep the outstanding

balance of your credit cards at less than half of your credit limit.

By that I mean if your card has a $500.00 limit, then keep the

credit balance at $250.00 or less at all times and your credit

score will improve. Second, don't allow people to constantly check your credit report. It will bring your credit score down. Bring your credit report with you. Third, pay your bills on time. Pay often, pay early and pay more than required if that is possible. If you can't pay more than what is required then pay the minimum amount on time. I think you should check your credit report at least twice a year and read it. Make sure no one is using your name or your credit cards. You can check your credit score for free by going to www.annualcreditreport.com. Also, the three credit bureaus Equifax, Transunion and Experian will provide a free credit report each year. There are other places where you can obtain a free credit report but these are the most respected. They will provide you with an accurate reading of your credit report. In the United States, the most widely used reporting company is Fair Isaac Corporation (FICO). It is a publicly traded company and very respected. The best credit score according to FICO is 850. The first step is to identify your credit score number. There are some companies out there that will give one free report but they want your credit card number first and then a commitment that you will check your score every year or twice a year. If you check your credit score, twice a year, then they will bill your credit card so be mindful. I think checking your credit score at least once every year is a great idea. If there is something on your credit report that should not be there, you can fix it; however, if there is something that happened in the last year at least you know what it is and you can fix it. Credit scoring is not limited to banks and cell phone companies. Today colleges are doing credit checks. If you want to get ahead with your education, you may have to pay for one class at time if you have bad credit. Landlords may check your credit before they rent an apartment to you. They can decline renting an apartment to you based on your credit. It is worth the effort to improve your credit. Just remember improving your credit is like losing weight it takes time. Start by paying your bills on time and take a look at your credit history. The information that has been on your credit report longer than seven years should go away. If the old information is not removed, then dispute it online on your credit report. Also you may write a letter to the credit reporting agency disputing the old information. If you write a letter or dispute the old information online with the credit reporting agency and the creditor doesn't respond within thirty days, the credit reporting agency must remove the information from your credit report.

Chapter Fourteen
Micro Loans

A title loan is where the borrower uses the title of his or her car as collateral for the loan. The loans are usually short term. What the lender does is use half of the book value of the car. Title loans tend to have higher interest rates than other sources of credit. The interest rates can be as high as 26%. The lenders don't require a credit check so they assume greater risk. Title loans are taken out mostly by people who are in a financial bind. A person can get a title loan in approximately 15 minutes. You can borrow anywhere from $100.00 to around $2,500.00. Most lenders won't lend more than that amount. Most financial institutions won't loan such a small amount of money because it is such a small amount and too risky for the lender. The title lender needs to make sure that you are employed and that your car is not older than eight years old. The car has to be in decent shape. As with anything, there are positives and negatives with title loans. The negative side of title loans is that many people have trouble repaying their loans. Many borrowers extend their loans into weeks making it a worse financial situation. Another negative of title loans is these loans are very expensive and few who take them out realize just how expensive. Instead of stating an annual rate, their contact says "finance fee" that is why the Chartered Financial Analyst (CFA) and the Federal Trade Commission (FTC) have declared title lending as a predatory lending or legal loan sharking based around The Truth In Lending Act. The Truth in Lending Act (TILA) is a federal law designed to promote consumer protection by requiring disclosure of terms, the cost of the loan and what those terms mean. Many lenders do abide by the law and you should try to find an honest lender so shop around. The positive side is you receive instant approval. For certain customers, these loans are a blessing. If it were not for payday lenders, these customers would have nowhere to go. If your only option is to bounce a check, remember each bounced check will cost you somewhere in the range of $20 to $35 dollars. A bounced check will affect your relationship with the bank. Also bounced checks may affect your credit rating as well. Payday loans are cheaper than a bounced check because the bank keeps charging a $30 fee every day until the debt is paid and you might not have the money. If the consumer understands how payday lending works, this can be the answer to your prayers. I see payday lenders predominately in the South but not so much in places like New York. I think it is because a car is more valuable in the South than in the North. You have to have a car in the South. Another reason that payday lenders are prevalent in the South is because payday lenders have powerful lobbyists who have prevented the regulations of the payday lending industry.

Remember to be mindful when you borrow from title loan companies and choose to borrow responsibly. A payday loan is not intended to go into infinity. Plus thanks to government regulation you can only roll over your payday loan so many times. If the loan is rolled over too many times and the lender has not been paid, the lender will repossess the car. The lender does not want the car because it could take months to find the car, and it takes time to sell the car.

Chapter 15
Running a Business

If someone told me thirty years ago that I could not run my own business I would have sock them right in the eye, kick them, and said don't tell me what I can't do. The truth is I have succeeded as much as I have failed. I have friends that work in board rooms at brokerage houses all over New York and that works for them. As for me, I love being in business for myself. I would not have it any other way. I live an all commission life. An all commission life means I do not receive a salary every week or every two weeks. I am paid commissions for the work that I do. There was a time I was a captured broker. A captured broker is someone who chooses to work in the board room of a bigger firm. Working in the board room is called being in the bull pin. When your work is commission only and things are going well you are rich, but when things are tough every move you make has to be thought out well. For people who open restaurants, convenience stores and card shops follow your dream. The glory is worth the effort. If you are going to start a business, please make sure that you file the proper papers to incorporate your business and protect yourself. There is nothing like going to your office in the morning, unlocking your door and getting down to business. In 2011, there are tax credits the IRS will give you if you hire people to help you run your business. For instance, the Affordable Care Act helps individuals and their families get affordable health care for the office. Providing healthcare insures that you will find and keep talented employees. The Small Business Jobs Act that President Obama signed into law recently is important because small businesses create most of the jobs in this country. One of the bonuses of owning a business is accelerated depreciation. This is a tax credit for businesses that invest in capital. This will help them recover their money quickly. Small businesses use carry back to increase cash flow for business by providing a 5 year carry back of net operating loss. Another plus of owning your own business is a tax credit for hiring recently discharged veterans and disconnected youths who have been out of school six months or more. Another privilege of owning a small business is pay roll tax deduction which provides businesses with exemptions from social security payroll tax for every worker hired since 2010 who been unemployed for at least 60 days. There are bonuses for keeping employee long term which provides an additional $1000.00 tax credit for every new worker retained for 52 weeks or more. There is a new small business lending bill which will provide $30 billion dollars for the Small Business Administration to lend to small banks with the incentive to increase lending to small businesses. I have provided you with an overview of the benefits of owning a small business. If you want more in depth information, it can be found

on the internet. My hope is if there is something in this book

that makes you think and you want to learn more you can.

Glossary

Common stock is a security that represents ownership in a corporation.

Bond is a debt investment in which an investor loans money to an entity either corporate or governmental that borrows the funds for a certain period of time at a fixed interest rate.

Insurance policy is a contact between the insurer and the insured.

Micro Credit (Micro Loans) is a very small loan for those

in need of cash right away.

Annuity is a contract that converts a sum of money into a series of periodic payments for an agreed upon period of time.

Stock broker is a regulated professional broker who buys

and sells stocks and other securities on behalf of an investor.

Financial Advisor is a person who renders financial services to individuals, businesses and governments. This can includes pension planning and/or life insurance.

Tax Sale is a sale of real property by a taxing authority to recover delinquent taxes.

Consumer is a broad label for any individual or household that uses goods and services generated within the economy.

Investment has different meanings in finance and economics. In finance, an investment is putting money into something with the expectation of gain.

Income Statement is a financial statement that measures a company's performance over a specific accounting period of time.

Balance Sheet is a financial statement that summarizes a

company's assets and liabilities and shareholders' equity over a

specific point and time.

Cash Flow Statement reports a company's inflow and outflow of

cash.